Little Pebble™

Celebrate Autumn

Harvest Time

by Erika L. Shores

raintree
a Capstone company — publishers for children

D0541911

Raintree is an imprint of Capstone Global Library Limited, a company incorporated in England and Wales having its registered office at 7 Pilgrim Street, London, EC4V 6LB – Registered company number: 6695582

www.raintree.co.uk
myorders@raintree.co.uk

Text © Capstone Global Library Limited 2016
The moral rights of the proprietor have been asserted.

Editorial Credits
Edited by Mari Bolte and Erika Shores
Designed by Cynthia Della-Rovere
Picture research by Svetlana Zhurkin
Production by Morgan Walters

ISBN 978 1 4747 0296 6 (hardback)
19 18 17 16 15
10 9 8 7 6 5 4 3 2 1

ISBN 978 1 4747 0301 7 (paperback)
20 19 18 17 16 15
10 9 8 7 6 5 4 3 2 1

Printed and Bound in China.

British Library Cataloguing in Publication Data
A full catalogue record for this book is available from the British Library.

Photo Credits
Dreamstime: Robin Van Olderen, 12, SandraRBarba, 6—7, Smellme, 16 (right); Newscom: ZUMA Press/Tony Crocetta, 26—27; Shutterstock: Aaron Amat, 27 (top), ala737, 13 (bottom), Alta Oosthuizen, 15 (top), 18, Ana Gram, 25, 29 (inset), bjogroet, 11 (top), Black Sheep Media (grass), throughout, Chantal de Bruijne (African landscape), back cover and throughout, creative, 10, e2dan, 13 (top), Eric Isselee, cover, back cover, 1, 4, 7 (top), 11 (bottom), 21 (top), 23 (top), 32, Gerrit_de_Vries, 14 (top), 17, Jez Bennett, 14 (bottom), John Michael Evan Potter, 9, Maggy Meyer, 28—29, MattiaATH, 8, Mogens Trolle, 15 (bottom), moizhusein, 20—21, 23, Moments by Mullineux, 5, Sean Stanton, 19, Serge Vero, 24, Stuart G. Porter, 22

Contents

On the farm

Autumn is here.

Farmers bring in crops.

A farmer uses a big machine.

It is called a combine harvester.

Corn grows in rows. Combines collect the cobs of corn.

In the garden

Look at the garden!
It is time to pick
vegetables.

Squash grows on vines.

Find a big one!

Grab a tomato.
Red tomatoes are
ready to eat.

Carrots grow underground. Pull them up.

Cabbage heads
are big and round.

The garden is empty. What will you plant next spring?

Glossary

combine harvester large farm machine used to gather corn and other crops from fields

crop plant farmers grow in large amounts, usually for food

harvest gather crops that are ripe

ripe ready to pick and eat

spring season after winter and before summer

vine plant with a long thin stem that grows along the ground or up a fence

Read more

A Nature Walk on the Farm (Nature Walks), Louise Spilsbury (Raintree, 2014)

What Can You See in Autumn? (Seasons), Sian Smith (Raintree, 2014)

Websites

www.bbc.co.uk/gardening/digin/your_space/patch.shtml
Celebrate autumn by growing and harvesting fruit and vegetables in your garden or on your windowsill. Follow the BBC's step-by-step picture guide to help you get started.

www.naturedetectives.org.uk/autumn/
Download wildlife ID sheets, pick up some great autumn crafting ideas and collect recipes for some delicious autumn cooking projects on this website.

Index